Ana Maria Pacheco

in the National Gallery

This book was published to accompany an exhibition at

THE NATIONAL GALLERY, LONDON
entitled *Ana Maria Pacheco in the National Gallery: New Painting and Sculpture*
29 September 1999 – 9 January 2000
Supported by The Bernard Sunley Charitable Foundation, The Henry Moore Foundation
and The Elephant Trust

and at

WOLVERHAMPTON ART GALLERY (January – April 2000)
GLYNN VIVIAN ART GALLERY, SWANSEA (April – June 2000)
WHITWORTH ART GALLERY, MANCHESTER (July – October 2000)
MAPPIN ART GALLERY, SHEFFIELD (October 2000 – January 2001)
BRIGHTON MUSEUM AND ART GALLERY (February – April 2001)

Ana Maria Pacheco is represented by Pratt Contemporary Art, England

First published in Great Britain in 1999 by
NATIONAL GALLERY PUBLICATIONS LIMITED
St Vincent House, 30 Orange Street, London WC2H 7HH

Reprinted 1999

ISBN 1 85709 274 0 paperback
525449

British Library Cataloguing-in-Publication Data.
A catalogue record is available from the British Library.

Editor: John Jervis
Art director: Andrew Gossett
Design & typesetting in Poliphilus & *Blado*: STUDIOGOSSETT

Front cover: Ana Maria Pacheco, *Luz Eterna* (detail), 1999
Back cover: Ana Maria Pacheco, *Dark Night of the Soul* (detail), 1999

Title page: Ana Maria Pacheco, *Queen of Sheba and King Solomon in the Garden of Earthly Delights*
(detail), 1999
Imprint page: Ana Maria Pacheco, *Queen of Sheba and King Solomon in the Garden of Earthly Delights*
(detail), 1999
Contents page: Ana Maria Pacheco, *Untitled Study for Sculpture*, 1998–9

Printed and bound in Great Britain by Jarrold Book Printing, Thetford, Norfolk

'The Ship of Death' © Laurence Pollinger Limited and the Estate of Frieda Lawrence Ravagli

Contents

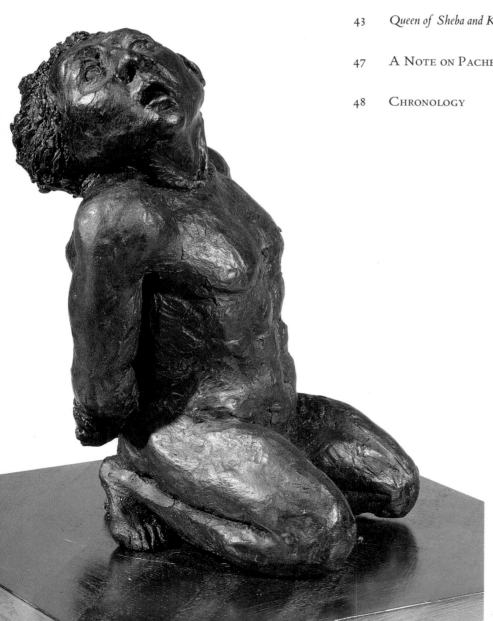

FOREWORD

Ana Maria Pacheco's studio at the National Gallery

Aɴᴀ Mᴀʀɪᴀ Pᴀᴄʜᴇᴄᴏ is the Gallery's fourth Associate Artist, and has been working in a studio in the Gallery for the past two years, making work that directly reflects on some of the great themes of the collection: metamorphosis; the struggles between good and evil; the narratives of Christianity and legends such as the story of Saint Sebastian.

Pacheco is the first Associate Artist who is not European. She was born in Brazil and her work reflects the rich diversity of a culture steeped in a Roman Catholic tradition, with an admixture of African art reminding one of the slave trade's links with Brazil, an art education system promoting international modernism, and a highly developed sense of national identity. In Pacheco's case, her long residence in Britain has added many other elements to the mixture, leading to a totally independent trajectory as an artist, unmoved by fashion.

Pacheco is also the first Associate Artist to be sculptor, painter and printmaker. She moves freely between media, and this exhibition develops themes in sculpture first explored in prints, new ideas generated by the experience of being in the Gallery, and long-matured thoughts about certain subjects – a fascination with mysterious containers, with severed heads, with mythic figures like the Sphinx.

The National Gallery has always been a resource for artists. The Associate Artist scheme makes it possible for one artist to delve deeply into the collection and to absorb the lessons of the art of the past on a daily basis. Ana Maria Pacheco's work shows how varied and powerful the results of such appropriation can be.

We are delighted to acknowledge the support of The Bernard Sunley Charitable Foundation, The Henry Moore Foundation and The Elephant Trust in making this exhibition possible.

Neil MacGregor
Dɪʀᴇᴄᴛᴏʀ

Pacheco working on *Dark Night of the Soul*

Terra Ignota
THE ART OF ANA MARIA PACHECO

Kathleen Adler

IN A DETAIL from the sequence of paintings *In Illo Tempore* ('In That Time'),
completed by Ana Maria Pacheco in 1994, a young girl wearing a light-yellow dress
with dazzling white ankle socks emerges from a background of alien beings, creatures
of the spirit world, creatures of darkness, figures from the world of carnival (FIG. 1).
The contrast between the youth of the girl, with her light clothing, suggestive of
virginity and innocence, and the shadowy darkness of the background is striking.
The child is standing on a simple podium, like that used by Pacheco for many of her
figures, and it is as if this podium protects her from the forces surrounding her. She is
represented as a figure at the margins, between innocence and experience, between the
rational and the world of 'blind' faith.

At one level it might be tempting to read such an image as redolent of all that makes
Ana Maria Pacheco's work 'Brazilian', yet this would be too simplistic and would
ignore that, although Pacheco neither would nor could deny her Brazilian roots, her
'Brazilian-ness', she does not define her identity primarily through being Brazilian.
Even so, as this image suggests, it is the very ambiguity of her relationship to her
Brazilian origins, and to the world of her childhood and early maturity, that lies
behind the work she produces. And it is the conflicts and contrasts suggested by this
image that lie at the heart of Pacheco's making of art.

Pacheco was born and brought up in Goiânia, in the state of Goiás, in the West
Central region of Brazil (FIG. 2). Goiás was for many years at the Brazilian frontier
with Spanish Paraguay, at the edges of the region dominated by Portugal. Formed by
adventurism and the quest for gold, it is now deep in the heartland of Brazil. The flag
of the state, diagonal stripes of green and yellow, marks this: the green stripes represent
the forests, and the yellow, the richness of gold. A blue oblong in the corner, with
silver stars, denotes the splendid skies of the southern hemisphere and the brilliance
of the Southern Cross constellation which gave Brazil its first names of 'Vera Cruz'
and 'Santa Cruz'. Goiás is a place on the boundary between the vast untamed
swampland of the Mato Grosso, the Pantanal, where even today many Indian tribes
still live, and the urban – Brazil's capital, Brasilia, founded in 1960, is 200 kilometres
away from Goiânia, and with its coming there has been a rapid expansion in the
region, but the population remains relatively sparse. Modern-day Goiânia is a town
with many tall buildings, and its centre looks almost like a North American city, but
it stands between the 'civilisation' of the twentieth century and far more ancient ways.
As recently as Pacheco's youth, wild pigs ran through the streets and leopards were
said to attack animals on neighbouring farms, while the swamplands are still full of
huge anacondas and alligators. Today, the contrast between the immensely powerful
landowning families, with their huge estates and their control over the power of the

1 *In Illo Tempore I* (detail), 1994
Oil on gesso, 183.4 × 260 cm
Birmingham Museums and Art Gallery

Catholic church, and the oppression of the peasantry results in the perpetuation of almost feudal relationships.

From early in her career, Pacheco was aware of the contradictions involved in being a modern artist in Brazil. The art school she attended at the University of Goiás was a place where, in the best colonial traditions, the focus was entirely on the narratives of European modernism, a history of twentieth-century art from Picasso to Pollock, and perhaps above all, a history of modern European art which stressed the importance of abstraction and constructivism. Much contemporary Brazilian art has followed the path of constructivism, but this was not a route that interested Pacheco. She would often emerge from her classes and look at the landscape surrounding the town, and wonder how to reconcile the world of European learning, particularly its emphasis on rationality, geometry and control, with the rawness of her surroundings, so little subject to such controls. It was at this time she began to make landscape sketches, a practice very much at odds with the teaching of the school. As she said to Ian Starsmore in 1989:

... when you leave the building [the university] you go out to confront this landscape and ecology that has nothing to do with what you have learned ... everything is thin, uncertain, distorted, scared and fearful like an animal hunted ... (Ian Starsmore, *"Inventing the Black Powder": Art and Education*, Pratt Contemporary Art, 1989)

Like many women of her generation, Pacheco had to struggle to convince others that she was serious about being an artist. Her father was supportive enough of art as an accomplishment, but wary of the idea of his daughter identifying herself as an artist in a society deeply conditioned to view women as wives and mothers. In time Pacheco convinced him, as she does with most people. She completed the degree of Bachelor of

2 Map of the area surrounding Goiânia, Brazil

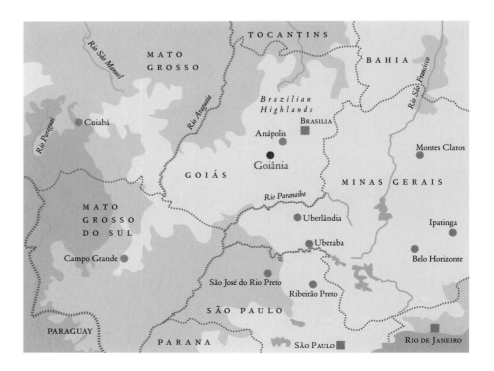

ANA MARIA PACHECO *in the National Gallery*

Arts in Sculpture at the University of Goiás, and a degree in music at the Federal University of Goiás, and then went to Rio de Janiero to study music and education. On her return to Goiás, she taught at the Institute of Education on a teacher training course, and at the Schools of Fine Arts and of Architecture at the University of Goiás, as well as at the Federal University of Goiás, until 1973. Her first major artistic breakthrough came in 1970 when she won first prize in the Goiás Biennale and was selected to represent Brazil at the São Paulo Biennale in the following year. This experience of combining her own practice with teaching proved useful when, in 1985, she became Head of Fine Art at the Norwich School of Art.

Pacheco was awarded a British Council Scholarship to the Slade School of Fine Art, London, in 1973. As so many foreign students coming to London have found, London was a place at once well known through literature, and deeply strange: colder, greyer, and smaller than it was possible to have imagined. Since then, Pacheco has been coming to terms with what it means to live always in a foreign country, to love it and want to stay, and yet for it to remain always alien. But it is from such conflicts and tensions that her art derives its strength, and a permanent return to Brazil does not seem an option.

Pacheco's work both as a sculptor and as a draughtsman and printmaker began to be recognised in the early 1980s. She showed at the Institute of Contemporary Arts, London, in the exhibition 'Women's Images of Men', and at exhibitions and biennales throughout Europe: in Rijeka, Yugoslavia; Cracow, Poland; and Fredrikstad, Norway. The Ikon Gallery in Birmingham showed her work – sculpture, drawings and prints – in 1983, and she held a residency at the linked Ikon Workspace for the duration of the exhibition. A year later, she was awarded an artist-in-school residency at Trinity School in Leamington Spa, Warwickshire.

3 *The Longest Journey*, 1994. Polychromed wood, 320 × 335 × 1000 cm

4 *Requiem*, 1986–95
Portland stone, slate, bronze and steel, 310 × 750 × 340 cm

5 & 6 *Requiem* (details), 1986–95

She has always enjoyed working with students, and the opportunity to do so on a more permanent basis came with her move to the Norwich School of Art in 1985. However the pressures of combining her own work with the administrative and personnel demands of running an art school led Pacheco to decide in 1989 to devote herself to her practice. Her work was displayed in many exhibitions, including a solo show at the Artsite Gallery and St John's Catholic Church in Bath in 1989–90, which toured extensively – to the Cornerhouse in Manchester, to Wolverhampton Art Gallery, and to Worcester Cathedral, among other venues. Her show of sculpture and drawings, 'Some Exercise of Power', was at the Camden Arts Centre, London, and the Museum of Modern Art in Oxford in 1991, and at the Oriel in Cardiff in 1992. In 1994 her huge sculpture, *The Longest Journey* (FIG. 3), was exhibited at the Gas Hall in the Birmingham Museum and Art Gallery, and the following year, her sculpture *Requiem* (FIG. 4) was sited at the Goodwood/Hat Hill Sculpture Foundation.

Requiem, now at the University of Essex, Colchester, is dominated by a monumental figure in Portland stone, stiff, staring rigidly ahead. The work's formality and associations with Egyptian or archaic Greek art are mitigated and made humorous by the red-and-white striped bathing trunks the figure wears. The figure is linked to a slate pyramid by two curving pieces of red metal. On the pyramid is a mysterious package, red, bound with rope (FIG. 6). It is this sense of mystery, of packages which if opened would be as threatening as Pandora's box, which dominates Pacheco's work. One could try to label such a sculpture as part surreal, part self-consciously 'primitive', but such labelling would only take one further from explaining its charge and force, its compelling mystery. In a sheet accompanying the first exhibition of this piece, the poet George Szirtes wrote: 'We play these games of association and form as if they were a riddle waiting for some Oedipal answer, and it is all we are going to get. Provisional riddles have provisional solutions. The final riddles one doesn't talk about.'

Dates and exhibition titles tell us of a career in the making, but they tell us nothing about the continuity of imagery in Pacheco's work, nor her struggle to establish a position for herself in the English art world. She has always worked against the grain. She has not sought to be identified as a 'Latin American magic realist', a label which would at least have given her a recognisable identity in this country. It is, however, a label which Pacheco finds meaningless in the context of the visual arts, although it may have some valid currency in literature. By remaining implacably committed to a figurative tradition, she has also been very much against the current of conceptual or minimalist art. But her relative isolation has, in some respects, been a huge advantage. It has enabled her to pursue ideas and themes over extended periods of time, to develop a body of work where the transitions between drawing, drypoint or etching, painting and sculpture can be explored, and where there are none of the pressures often brought to bear on artists by dealers, anxious to promote new 'isms' or to persuade their artists to repeat a winning formula.

7 *Study for Saint Sebastian I*, 1998. Drypoint, plate size 79.8 × 59.8 cm

ANA MARIA PACHECO *in the National Gallery*

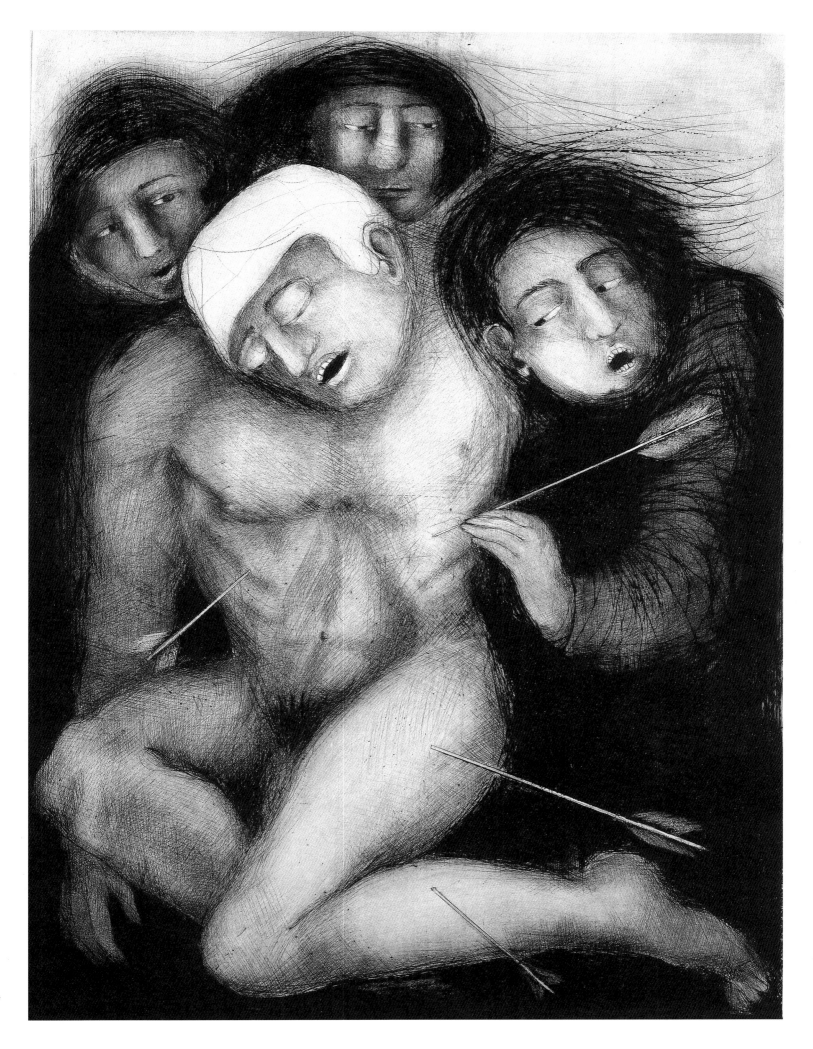

Terra Ignota: THE ART OF ANA MARIA PACHECO

Pacheco moves freely between one medium and another. While she is doing a drawing, it may also form the basis of an etching or may suggest development as a sculpture, even while it retains its own integrity. The crossovers between different mediums are a source of great creative strength to her, and she sometimes works out the solution to a problem in one medium by engaging with another medium and another theme, albeit often a closely related one. Pacheco brings to her art an intricate cultural baggage. She trained as a musician and music is deeply important to her – she always has music playing while she works. She is steeped in the Bible, the classics of European culture, and the writings of the Greeks and Romans – Ovid's *Metamorphoses* has been a key text for her – and she reads and looks extremely widely. The Saint Sebastian theme, at the heart of this exhibition (FIG. 7), evolves from what David Elliott has called a 'chronicle of riddles, journeys, secrets, temptations, seductions and death' ('The Smile on the Face of the Tiger', *In Illo Tempore*, Pratt Contemporary Art, 1994). The violence of the theme is something at the core of much of Pacheco's work: a rich blend of Catholicism and of the myriad other influences that play their part in the development of Brazilian culture.

Brazil is a country where ninety per cent of the population define themselves as Roman Catholic, and the force of this is very evident in the enduring strength of a tradition of Baroque architecture and sculpture. There are also vestiges of West African artistic traditions brought to Brazil by the many thousands of slaves who were sent there at the height of the slave traffic. One of Pacheco's pieces, the *Study of Head (John the Baptist III)* (FIG. 8), vividly demonstrates these different traditions. The theme is a favourite one in Baroque art, but the charring of the wood suggests Yoruba sculpture from the west coast of Africa, while the addition of porcelain teeth combines both these traditions – the teeth often found in African masks and the teeth to be found on figures sculpted by Brazil's Baroque sculptors. Even with a theme as ostensibly part of the canonical western European tradition as Saint Sebastian, there

8 *Study of Head (John the Baptist III)*, 1992

Polychromed wood, 31.8 × 50.8 × 74 cm (exc. base)

ANA MARIA PACHECO *in the National Gallery*

9 Antônio Francisco Lisboa, *The Last Supper*, 1796–9
Congonhas, Bom Jesus de Matosinhos

are never straightforward allusions to specific paintings and sculptures from this tradition in Pacheco's work – as Colin Wiggins discusses on page 25 the references are often to photography or to cinema. Saint Sebastian, patron saint of Rio de Janeiro, victim of and victor over the archers' arrows, often portrayed as a highly androgynous figure, is an ideal subject for the subtleties of Pacheco's approach.

Brazilian art has, however, played a vital part in the development of her work, in particular the Baroque art which adorns such Brazilian churches as the Chapel of the Third Order of Saint Francis of Assisi in Ouro Preto, with its elaborate iconography and sculpted heads. The work of one of the artists at Ouro Preto, O Aleijadinho (The Little Cripple), has been very important to her – Antônio Francisco Lisboa, Brazil's most important Baroque sculptor, was born in the 1730s, and trained by his father, the Portuguese architect Manuel Francisco Lisboa. His mother was a Creole, descended from the original Portuguese settlers, called Isabel. He worked as an architect, designer, and sculptor. For the last three decades of his life, he suffered from an illness which disfigured his body and almost blinded him, hence his nickname by which he is best known. Perhaps the most important of his works are the *Twelve Prophets* in the courtyard of the Church of Bom Jesus at Congonhas, made between 1800 and 1805, and the more than sixty wooden figures which constitute the *Stations of the Cross* on the Via Sacra outside the church, sculpted a few years earlier, between 1796 and 1799 (FIG. 9). These works were made from cedar, and were painted later by Manuel da Costa Ataíde, the most important painter of the 'Mineiro' period of Brazilian history, during the reign of Maria I (1777–1816), and at the height of the gold and diamond rush in Brazil. The sacred figures are painted in pastel tones, the tormentors of Christ in strong colours. Glass eyes were added at a later period. The polychromy was restored in 1957, and the impact of the whole on Pacheco's vividly coloured wooden figures is strong.

Terra Ignota: THE ART OF ANA MARIA PACHECO

10 *Between Mitcham and Croydon: the Heritage of the Aged*, 1977

Etching, plate size 44 × 55 cm

She adds to these influences a familiarity with Brazilian myths and legends, often closely related to their European counterparts, particularly the fables of Aesop, and the fairy tales of the brothers Grimm and Hans Christian Andersen, all well known in Brazil. As with Pacheco's art, in these Brazilian variants on European fables there is always a twist on a tale we may think we know: the animals may be tapirs rather than European animals – the familiarity of, say, hare and tortoise, is transformed. Such fables, with their settings of terrifying forests (or jungles), their morals, and their transgression of the rational order, are very important to Pacheco and her exploration of the unfamiliar, the unknown, the uncharted territories of the subconscious. She constantly seeks to move into what the Portuguese call '*terra ignota*', undiscovered country, and to risk what she will find there. The metaphor of the journey is strong in her work, running through it as a leitmotif.

Ana Maria Pacheco *in the National Gallery*

12 *Terra Ignota 2*, 1993. Drypoint, plate size 32.5 × 25.4 cm

13 *Terra Ignota 5*, 1993. Drypoint, plate size 32.5 × 25.4 cm

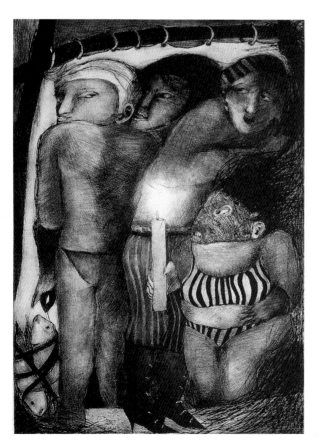

11 *The Longest Journey I*, 1987
Drypoint, plate size 108.5 × 72.5 cm

In 1977 Pacheco produced a series of etchings based on a regular bus journey, *Between Mitcham and Croydon: the Heritage of the Aged* (FIG. 10). The figures who make this prosaic journey are transformed into what can only be called 'Pacheco people', on a quest for who knows what, far removed from the commonplace, light years from South London's suburbs. The theme of the journey continued ten years later with two large drypoints from 1987, *The Longest Journey I* (FIG. 11) and *II*, and again three years later in *Perils of the Faith 2*, and in the series of ten drypoints of 1993, *Terra Ignota*. In the latter series, masked figures in small boats travel across dark indeterminate spaces (FIG. 12), or find themselves suspended over creatures of myth, such as the rhinoceros who appears in *Terra Ignota 5* (FIG. 13) – not a South American animal, this beast appears more as a reference to strangeness than to an actual creature.

Terra Ignota: THE ART OF ANA MARIA PACHECO

14 *The Longest Journey*, 1994. Polychromed wood, 320 × 335 × 1000 cm

15 *The Longest Journey* (detail), 1994

The theme of the journey was developed in the large sculptural group, *The Longest Journey* (FIG. 14), of 1994. In a wooden boat, ten metres long, many figures cluster. Some wear the cap seen often in Pacheco's work, a combination of a ceremonial helmet and a swimming cap. The children wear striped T-shirts, while two of the women wear elaborately carved and polychromed dresses. The other five figures, far more ambiguous, wear long cloak-like garments, which strongly retain the sense of the wood from which they are made. The longest journey is of course the journey towards death, but in another sense it is life itself, and in these polychromed wooden figures, with their teeth made by dentists to mimic the imperfections of real teeth, and their range of expressions, Pacheco has captured something of the rich variety of human life. This vessel may be a Ship of Fools, but equally, perhaps it is an Ark, with its promise of redemption. Szirtes in his essay on *The Longest Journey* (Pratt Contemporary Art, 1996) quotes D.H. Lawrence's poem 'The Ship of Death' from his *Last Poems*, published in 1932:

ANA MARIA PACHECO *in the National Gallery*

16 & 17 *The Longest Journey* (details), 1994

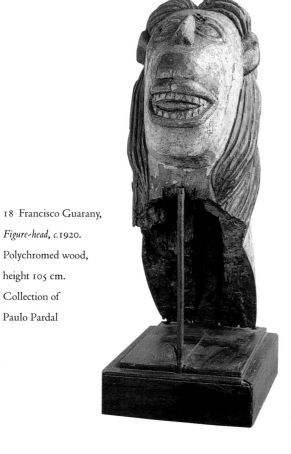

18 Francisco Guarany,
*Figure-head, c.*1920.
Polychromed wood,
height 105 cm.
Collection of
Paulo Pardal

And the little ship wings home, faltering and lapsing
on the pink flood,
and the frail soul steps out, into her house again …

Pacheco has been very struck by a series of boats with mask-like figure-heads made by the sculptor Francisco Guarany, who was born in 1882 and died at the age of 103 in 1985. These masks, carved from the early 1900s until about the 1940s, are of human and animal heads, made of cedar and polychromed (FIG. 18). They are intended to protect boats on their journeys – the explorer Jacques Cousteau had a two-metre high Guarany mask on his boat, the *Calypso*, on his Amazon expedition. They also exist as works of art in their own right, and, like many of Pacheco's works, evoke ancient Egypt as well as Brazilian traditions. Works by Pacheco like the *Box of Heads* of 1983 (FIG. 19) and the *Studies of Heads* of 1986 have much of the same qualities of the grotesque, the terrifying, and the humorous that are to be found in Guarany's work.

Terra Ignota: THE ART OF ANA MARIA PACHECO

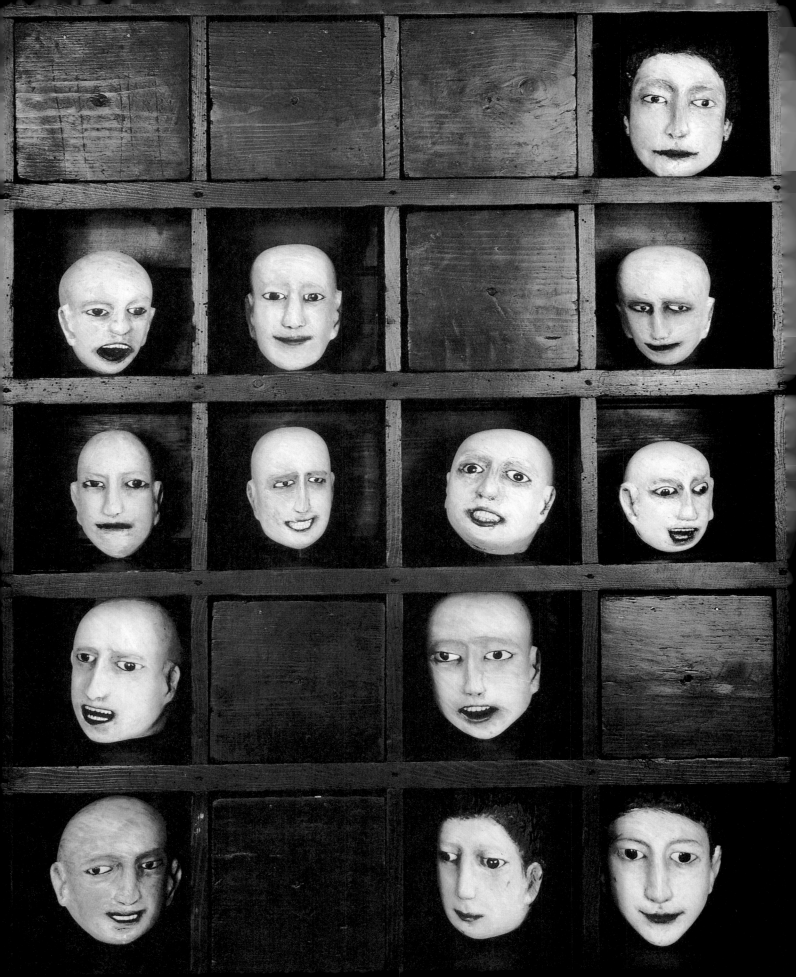

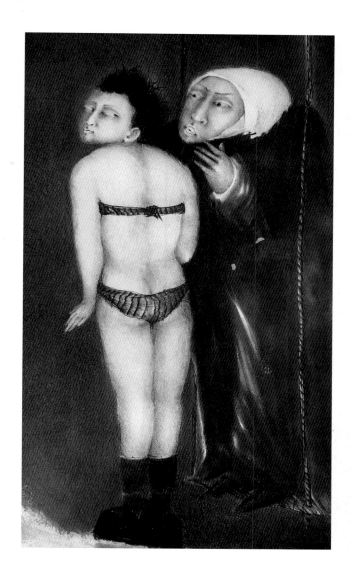

20 *Beheaded (Judith)* (detail, above), 1991
Charcoal, graphite and pastel on paper, 167.5 × 243.5 cm

21 *Beheaded (Salome)* (detail, above right), 1991
Charcoal, graphite and pastel on paper, 164.5 × 239.5 cm
Private Collection

19 *Box of Heads* (left), 1983
Polychromed wood, 93 × 71 × 20.3 cm
South East Arts Collection

The severed head is another of Pacheco's themes, as in the series *Memoria Roubada* ('Memories of plunder') of 1992, where one head in the series is hanging from a rope, while another is spiked. The pictorial language is that of Catholic imagery, but the meanings extend to an exploration of the theme of Brazil's colonial and post-colonial history of violence, ruthless exploitation, and brutality. In a much earlier series of etchings, dating from 1981, *Every Man Wears a Head on his Shoulder*, the source is a musical one, Penderecki's opera *The Devils of Loudun*, in which a surgeon and a chemist buy the head of a criminal after the body has been cut down from the gallows. Some of the themes of beheading are more familiar: both Judith and Salome are frequent subjects in Pacheco's work. Both are women who make use of their sexual power, and, as in so much of Pacheco's work, there is a fascination with overturning the traditional roles of victim and victor. *Beheaded (Judith)* of 1991 (FIG. 20), a drawing for a painting, shows Judith as a thoroughly modern woman, a figure from a beauty contest wearing a bathing suit and high-heeled shoes, perched on a pedestal – but she has a knife in her right hand, and in her left she holds another of Pacheco's mysterious packages, although this time we know that it contains the head of Holofernes. The facial expression is one of sly triumph. In *Beheaded (Salome)* (FIG. 21), Herodias descends on a trapeze to whisper into the bikini-clad Salome's ear – the variations on swimwear in Pacheco's art could be the subject of a whole essay in themselves.

Terra Ignota: THE ART OF ANA MARIA PACHECO

22 Unknown artist, reverse of *The Wilton Diptych* (detail),
about 1395–9. Egg (identified) on oak, 53 × 37 cm
London, National Gallery

23 *Tales of Transformations 3*, 1997–8. Drypoint, plate size 17.5 × 20 cm

25 *In Illo Tempore IV*, 1994. Oil on gesso, 260 × 183.4 cm

24 *Study for Transformations (V)* (detail), 1997
Oil pastel on paper, 52 × 66 cm
Private Collection

The themes of journeys and of severed heads are also about metamorphosis. The cycle
from birth to death is a cycle of change, and it is such change that fascinates Pacheco.
In bringing together, characteristically, the *Metamorphoses* of Ovid with Brazilian folk
tales about change, Pacheco's rich heritage is vividly manifest. In her *Tales of
Transformations*, one source is a Brazilian folk story about a medicine man who turns a
tribesman into a tapir which is, in turn, killed and eaten. The women of the village
are angry and jump into the river (FIG. 23), where they are turned into fishes, but,
in another phase of the story, they agree that the men of the village can fish them from
the river and turn them back into women. Another dimension of this story is that the
word for tapir, '*anta*', is also used in Portuguese to refer to stubborn and coarse women.
The same sequence of colour etchings also includes Medea driving her chariot,
drawn by three dragons, and a variant on the theme of Saint Hubert converting to
Christianity on seeing a stag with a crucifix between its antlers. In Pacheco's image,
the man is naked, like an Indian tribesman, and, beyond the wounded stag (FIG. 24)
with its reference to the white stag, King Richard II's personal emblem, in the
National Gallery's *Wilton Diptych* (FIG. 22), is the wonderful sky of Pacheco's native
Brazil, with the stars of the 'Santa Cruz' or Southern Cross.

ANA MARIA PACHECO *in the National Gallery*

26 *In Illo Tempore X*, 1994

Oil on gesso, 183.4 × 260 cm

Transformation is a theme too in the series *In Illo Tempore*, sometimes through the use of masks, such as the ram's head on the figure wearing a leopard- or ocelot-skin coat in *In Illo Tempore IV* (FIG. 25). In this scene, as in others from the sequence, the theme of the journey is also strong: the women stand on a wheeled platform, a crude thing like a child's soapbox, as much at odds with the conventional 'glamour' of the woman's apparel as the ram's head. This cart is apparently drawn by almost invisible gold threads, while, as in *Requiem* (FIG. 4), another mysterious package, a golden sack, is attached by other threads above the head of the companion figure, a woman in a green bathing suit. In the last of this sequence (FIG. 26), a cluster of figures is crammed into a wooden cart, drawn, it would seem, by a flying tapir ridden by a blindfolded woman. No wonder the woman in blue in the centre of the image looks apprehensive, crammed against a crowd of masked figures, dependent on this odd form of transport!

The look of apprehension is a familiar one in Pacheco's work, often expressed by the gesture of putting a hand to the lips, or by the mouth open in wonderment, as here in this painting from the *Memoria Roubada* sequence (FIG. 27). Here too the thin golden threads play a part, suspending the tapir from a rod, while the attitudes of the figures

Ana Maria Pacheco *in the National Gallery*

are reminiscent of the spectators in Goya's famous bullfighting images, and the masks hark back to Pietro Longhi and other Venetian depictions of carnival. It is such density of meaning that makes Pacheco's work so remarkable, such a blend of new world and old, of the traditions of western European art and the rawness of the history of conquest and pillage in the southern hemisphere. And one of the things Pacheco's art does, powerfully relevant for her work as Associate Artist at the National Gallery, is to remind us that it is not the southern hemisphere that has the prerogative on violence.

Seeing Pacheco's work in the context of the National Gallery, with its Collection of masterpieces of western European art, from the mid-thirteenth to the late nineteenth centuries, is a reminder of the force and intensity of the Gallery's paintings, a force sometimes neutralised by their presence in a museum of art, beautifully framed, hung and lit. Looking at the National Gallery's Collection again, after looking at Pacheco's work, serves to remind us how it too explores the themes of violence, death and love, how it too is about transformation and metamorphosis and journeys. The *terra ignota* of Ana Maria Pacheco's art is the unknown territory of all true art, and a willingness to plunge into this unknown and dangerous territory is the mark of a true artist.

Working at the National Gallery

Colin Wiggins

28 *Dark Night of the Soul* (detail), 1999

'I DON'T LIKE TO MAKE ART ABOUT ART', says Ana Maria Pacheco. Yet that is exactly how this exhibition has come about. In 1997 Pacheco accepted the National Gallery's invitation to become the fourth Associate Artist, and the first sculptor to participate in a scheme that carries with it the requirement of making new work directly inspired by the Gallery's Collection of paintings.

At the time of the Gallery's foundation in 1824, one of the stated reasons for its existence was to make great examples of European paintings available to contemporary artists in order that they might both learn from and be inspired by these works – the copying of acknowledged masterpieces of western European art was a necessary part of a young artist's education. Although this is no longer the case, this idea persists in the practice of reworking the art of the past. Picasso is a prime example of an artist who used work by other artists as a direct stimulus for his own work, most notably in his many versions of Velázquez's *Las Meninas*.

However, Pacheco outlines the problems that she perceives with such a concept. 'We are living at the end of the twentieth century and we cannot ignore history. But then there comes the constant danger of pastiche. The challenge from the past lies in being aware of the time that we live in. After Cubism, how can you sit down and do scientific perspective? And that is a major change because the world has changed. This is not to dismiss perspective or to say that painting is dead but it is no longer something that you yourself are discovering. You already know it, it does not have the potential that it had in the past. It's like making an explosion with black powder. You can't invent it any more. That poses a much harder question because someone else has done it. That is why it is problematic to copy others, because there's no big deal, you are not taking responsibility.'

Ana Maria Pacheco is the first non-European artist to have become so closely involved with this exclusively European Collection, having worked in the Gallery as Associate Artist for over two years. 'Coming from a colonial country, a mixture of cultures that forms a very thick soup, I don't carry the baggage of someone born in Europe', she says. Her approach has not been to look for compositions or other formal devices that she can use in her work, but to concentrate on studying some of the subjects and themes that have been dealt with by the artists in the Collection, and engage with them using her own cultural background and experience. The use of deliberate quotations from the work of other artists has been a common feature of European art since the Renaissance but it is unusual for Pacheco to do this. Instead, she consistently makes direct use of photo-journalism and cinema, sources that are uncompromisingly contemporary and little to do with the Old Master tradition.

29 *Dark Night of the Soul* (detail), 1999

Dark Night of the Soul

30 Antonio and Piero del Pollaiuolo, *The Martyrdom of Saint Sebastian*, completed 1475. Oil (identified) on poplar, 291.5 × 202.6 cm. London, National Gallery

31 *The Dark Night of the Soul*, 1993
Drypoint, plate size 108 × 82 cm

THE MOST SUBSTANTIAL WORK that has resulted from the Associateship is a multi-piece figure sculpture, *Dark Night of the Soul*. This sculpture was finally completed shortly before the exhibition and, owing to printing deadlines, only some of the figures can be illustrated here, along with the work in progress. The figures are all carved from wood and are free-standing. The main character is a kneeling and hooded man who is naked and transfixed with arrows (FIGS. 29, 37 & 38). He is surrounded by groups of onlookers. The theme is closely related to that most traditional of Renaissance subjects, the Martyrdom of Saint Sebastian, although by entitling her piece *Dark Night of the Soul*, a quotation from the Spanish mystic Saint John of the Cross, Pacheco eliminates any direct reference to Sebastian himself. She emphasises that this is not a representation of the early Christian saint, and is at pains to point out that she does not want the piece to be understood as exclusively Christian.

However, the undeniable reference to Sebastian initially forces us to consider Pacheco's choice of subject as being set within a traditional European framework. Sebastian was a Roman archer in the service of the Emperor Diocletian. He converted to Christianity, and as punishment, the Emperor had him shot through with arrows fired by his fellow archers. The customary iconography of Saint Sebastian shows him standing upright, bound to a tree or column, and certainly never blindfolded or hooded. A good example is the celebrated altarpiece by the Pollaiuolo brothers (FIG. 30) completed in 1475, now in the National Gallery, where the Saint turns his eyes towards heaven. This painting has long been a favourite of Pacheco's, and is one of the most direct inspirations for *Dark Night of the Soul*.

When the Gallery first approached Pacheco concerning the Associate Artist scheme in 1996, she was already working on this subject. Ten small panels (FIG. 32) had been made, each showing a solitary bound man shot through with arrows, in one of ten different positions. These were made as a way of working through the different possibilities of depicting such a figure and finding a pose that was distant from traditional representations. Radical devices such as the kneeling pose and the blindfold break away from the European past. Sebastian's usual standing position hints at fortitude and triumph, whereas Pacheco's final hooded man is both subjugated and humiliated. The figure made his first appearance in Pacheco's work in a large drypoint, *The Dark Night of the Soul*, of 1993 (FIG. 31). At this time there was no reference to the Saint Sebastian story – it was only later that Pacheco decided to re-use both figure and title in her new sculpture.

32 *Untitled Studies*, 1996. Oil on gesso, 59 × 102 cm

ANA MARIA PACHECO *in the National Gallery*

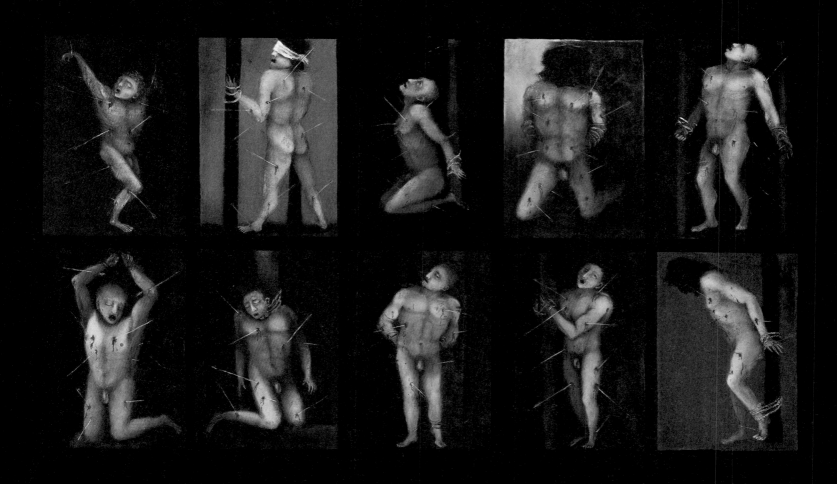

33 & 34 *Dark Night of the Soul* (details), 1999

35 Robert Mapplethorpe, *Hooded Man*, 1980

36 Carlos Humberto, *Death squad victim*, 1988

Apart from the victim, the only other naked figure in *Dark Night of the Soul* is a child, whose innocence is being abruptly ended by what he sees. Many of the other onlookers surrounding the victim seem largely passive and indifferent, as if they have seen it all before. There is a variety of implied responses, ranging from the sympathetic to the conspiratorial – maybe some of the characters are relieved that it not them tied to the post. The archers themselves also may be amongst the crowd, their duty done and their weapons put away. A group of young men, all similarly attired, look thuggish and very capable of committing this atrocity. But as the artist says, 'the actual executioners are just an agency of something that's far more powerful, which is those that cause the whole thing. It is they who are the ones who are dangerous.'

Viewers of the sculpture join these carved spectators in looking at, and responding to, the tortured victim. Perhaps there is an implication of our own passive role in inflicting the suffering on the victim. Pacheco's background has led her to have a strong interest in art of the Roman Catholic Counter-Reformation, with its tradition of confronting the spectator with the image of the suffering Christ or the martyred saints. Part of the purpose of work of this type was to make the viewers feel themselves responsible for causing the suffering. The active role of the viewer in Counter-Reformation art is at its most immediate with sculpture, where representations of suffering figures occupy the same physical space as the viewers, forcing them to participate.

Aside from Christian imagery, Pacheco has drawn on two other significant sources for *Dark Night of the Soul*, both from photography. The first is the work of Robert Mapplethorpe, homoerotic images of bondage that show tied and naked figures, exclusively black, photographed by a white artist (FIG. 35). The second is a photograph of an executed Brazilian bandit, his kneeling corpse garrotted and bound cruelly to a wooden post (FIG. 36). Events of this kind are tragically commonplace, especially, although not uniquely, in Latin America, yet this image elevates its nameless victim to an almost Christ-like status.

The facial types of Pacheco's figures are manifestly non-European, with elements such as the little porcelain teeth deriving from work produced by cultures once classified by the west as intimately bound up with the 'primitive'. She borrows a western theme, that of Saint Sebastian, but recasts it in her own language. A Christian martyrdom has become a pagan ritual. Her tortured figure is no longer specifically Sebastian but can be seen as a symbol of the martyrdom of colonised countries to western values. *Dark Night of the Soul*, with its Third World references, displayed in a safely western context, implicates spectators, through their own indifference, in the plight of colonised peoples and their historic exploitation by the west. But Pacheco is at pains not to allow such an interpretation to be overstated. 'I'm not trying to make a pamphlet kind of art that is connected with contemporary events. I'm much more interested in a particular sort of condition of humanity, or inhumanity.'

Pacheco's sculptural technique is remarkably direct. It has never been part of her method to make maquettes, small scale models of the sort employed by many artists, for example Henry Moore, before starting work on an actual sculpture. Pacheco's

ANA MARIA PACHECO *in the National Gallery*

37 *Dark Night of the Soul* (detail), 1999

39 *Study for Saint Sebastian II*, 1998
Drypoint, plate size 79.8 × 59.8 cm

38 *Dark Night of the Soul* (detail), 1999
Polychromed wood, height of figure 165 cm

figures can change, often quite dramatically, during the process of carving. 'I know of course the structure of the composition, but how it's going to evolve, I don't know. That's why I don't make models, because otherwise it would just be a design. You'd be dealing with what you know. In the visual arts you have to deal with what you don't know.'

However, experiments in print-making do form a part of her sculptural preparation. Pacheco's prints of Sebastian (FIGS. 7 & 39) take as their subject a different part of the saint's story. His ordeal with the arrows did not actually kill him. He was rescued and brought back to health by another early Christian saint, Irene, before he was finally martyred by being beaten to death with clubs. This crudely violent end to the story is rarely illustrated, with artists drawn to the more visually dramatic arrow scene. The Irene legend, however, has not infrequently been depicted, with the unconscious Sebastian slumped against his tree stump or column, being tended by his rescuer, and it is this scene that Pacheco has represented with two large drypoints.

Treating this part of the Sebastian story in a two-dimensional medium was an important part of the procedure of making the sculpture. 'I am a sculptor. Print-making and painting allow me to circumnavigate what I want to do finally in sculpture. I'm using a very traditional process of carving and today, with all the equipment that we now have, it's not particularly slow. However, it's the mental process that's slow for me and I think the reason is because sculpture is not that flexible. You can change the composition of a painting or a print. But with sculpture, at least the way I do it, it is very restricted. Apart from anything else, you are dealing with the space that you actually live in, a chair for example, or a fridge, occupies that same space. That creates an enormous difficulty for you to break through the visible world to the world one wants to deal with, that is the invisible.'

The two prints have enormous sculptural implications, with figures emphatically occupying space. Compositionally they bear no resemblance to the sculpture, but the experience of articulating these bodies in an illusionistic space feeds into the intellectual process of composing the sculpture.

40 *Dark Night of the Soul* (detail), 1999. Polychromed wood, height of figure 137 cm

41 *Untitled Studies for Sculpture*, 1998–9. Bronze, height ranging from 23 to 30.5 cm

ANA MARIA PACHECO *in the National Gallery*

A set of six small bronze figures (FIG. 41) also came out of this process, almost as a by-product. Pacheco made a set of the figures from clay, around 12 inches high, modelling rather than carving, as first thoughts for the finished wooden sculpture. They are not maquettes but approximations, initial ideas of how the figures are to look. They were made as guides for an assistant to bring the logs to a stage when Pacheco could start carving. The work done by the assistant, using a chain saw, consisted of blocking out the basic forms, and can be seen in a photograph taken in December 1998 (FIG. 43). The small clay figures were later cast in bronze, a process that Pacheco has resisted for her previous work – these bronzes have been made for this exhibition as demonstrations of her working process.

42 *Dark Night of the Soul* (detail), work in progress, June 1999

43 Photograph taken in December 1998 during the carving of *Dark Night of the Soul* – only the figure in the foreground has been substantially worked on by Pacheco.

Luz Eterna

LUZ ETERNA is a large scale triptych (FIG. 46), a format used for Renaissance altarpieces and successfully revived in the twentieth century by artists such as Max Beckmann and Francis Bacon. The title is in Portuguese, and translates as 'eternal light', a quotation from the Requiem Mass. The subject is a reworking of the story of Saint Anthony, a theme that has provided fertile ground for western artists from the medieval period to Cézanne in the nineteenth century. Pacheco's specific sources are a painting by Hieronymus Bosch in Lisbon (FIGS. 44 & 45) and Gustave Flaubert's *La Tentation de Saint Antoine*, published in 1874.

Anthony was a historical figure, whose story has been supplemented by many legends. He was a hermit who went into self-imposed exile for thirty years in the desert, in order to bring himself closer to God. During this time he was subjected to various visions, which included sexual temptation and being tormented by demons.

It was Pacheco's long-standing interest in the theme of exile, as a Brazilian working in Europe, that attracted her to this story. Another reason for her fascination with Anthony is the legend of his visions. 'It is the idea of hallucination that interests me, although his visions were not interpreted as such by theologians. I like to think that at the end of the twentieth century, after Freud, we have to read them with some added awareness. I like the idea that he transcended his level of consciousness and he could get into another world and would have visions. I think that is fascinating.'

44 Hieronymus Bosch
The Temptation of Saint Anthony (detail), *c.*1510

46 *Luz Eterna* (opposite), 1999
47 *Luz Eterna* (left panel, page 36), 1999. Oil on gesso, 259 × 183 cm
48 *Luz Eterna* (central panel, page 37), 1999. Oil on gesso, 259 × 183 cm

45 Hieronymus Bosch, *The Temptation of Saint Anthony*, *c.*1510
Oil on panel, 131.5 × 225 cm
Lisbon, Museu Nacional de Arte Antiga

ANA MARIA PACHECO *in the National Gallery*

The brickwork setting of the left-hand panel (FIG. 47), with its iron catwalk along the top, complete with surveillance camera, is a direct and literal representation of an internal courtyard of the National Gallery that is visible from Pacheco's studio. This dungeon-like setting becomes a metaphor for the dark corners of Anthony's mind. 'Or even', says Pacheco, 'the artist's own mind.' Furthermore, the inclusion of the sinister eye of the camera forcibly locates this image as set within our own time.

On one level, Pacheco turning a National Gallery courtyard into a terrifying, dark dungeon works as a joke, but on another level it also transforms the Gallery, or rather, what it stands for, into a dungeon. Today's artists can find themselves imprisoned by the massive heritage that the Collection represents, and it is incumbent upon them to break free. Pacheco's method of doing this has been to try and find a new language to deal with themes and subjects found in the Gallery's paintings.

Bosch's version of the story of Saint Anthony, now in Lisbon, is a painting that has long fascinated Pacheco. The three figures in her left-hand panel derive very loosely from a corner of the Bosch painting, in which monks are holding the saint after one of his visions (FIG. 44). There are also echoes of traditional western compositions of Christ being taken down from the Cross, although Pacheco's central figure is not dead but semi-conscious and suffering. The supporting figures are ambiguous – they might be there solely for the task of helping the hallucinating man but could in fact be responsible for his anguish. This reading is reinforced by the dark setting of the scene, which implies that the two figures could be jailers or torturers, and again by the starkly modern device of the camera.

The central panel is an uncompromisingly twentieth-century interpretation of the demons seen by Anthony (FIG. 48). Within the saint's story, these demons represent darkness, the devil and the pagan world that he struggled against. In the bottom part of Pacheco's picture a crowd cowers in fear from the menace above. The dark, swarming, diabolical shapes now take the form of helicopters, their sinister silhouettes transforming them into terrifying creatures of destruction.

An important influence on Pacheco's painting is film. 'Because of being brought up in Brazil, where there was such a great demand for them, I've seen all those old American films. It was much later when I started to paint and it is only now that I have started to see the connection. I think that for my generation, films have had a profound effect on the way we see things. Film, I think, is more akin to painting and theatre is more akin to sculpture. I remember seeing a film of Bergman's, *Through a Glass Darkly*, which is an excellent film. Funnily enough it's about madness, a woman having delusions, so there's certainly a connection here. I saw it over twenty-five years ago and what I retained was the memory of the emotion of the final scene. A helicopter comes down to pick up this woman because she's on an island and very sick. When it comes, it's against this white sky, this dark thing coming down. But my memory of it is much more dramatic, and I think it was my heightened emotion that I remember. When I saw the film again recently it was not exactly what I had remembered.'

49 *Luz Eterna* (right panel), 1999
Oil on gesso, 259 × 183 cm

50 Titian, *Assumption of the Virgin*, 1516–18
Oil on panel, 690 × 360 cm. Venice, Santa Maria Gloriosa dei Frari

51 Dirck van Baburen, *Prometheus chained*, 1623
Oil on canvas, 202 × 184 cm. Amsterdam, Rijksmuseum

Pacheco's use of helicopters, as with her use of the photograph of a garrotted bandit for her *Dark Night of the Soul* sculpture, brings a traditional subject into the contemporary world. It also forges a direct link between the fear of hell that was ever-present in the medieval period and the fears that have replaced it in our own time.

'I wanted to represent the horror that the medieval mind felt at the idea of demons. Up above, there is heaven and light, while below there is hell and darkness. Despite the fact that we no longer believe this, it is still in the language and psychologically we still see things like that. Something that comes from above is traditionally good and benevolent and spiritual. If, however, you have a malignant thing that normally inhabits the darkness, coming from above and flying, then the fear must be immense. As we don't believe in demons any more, I thought here is something worse, these machines that can kill, that are so extraordinarily sophisticated there is no escape.'

The composition of this panel is strongly reminiscent of traditional representations of the Assumption of the Virgin, most especially the celebrated version by Titian in Santa Maria Gloriosa dei Frari, Venice (FIG. 50). But Pacheco has subverted the notion of flying upwards towards heaven, and has replaced it with a deadly downwards swooping motion. This has the effect of bringing to the painting a specifically twentieth-century meaning, as innocent victims such as a mother with a young child anticipate their destruction. Most poignant is the couple on the left, an old man and a young woman, possibly his daughter. They add a note of silence to the picture, in powerful contrast to the overwhelming mechanical whirring implied in the rest of the panel. They await their violent and undeserved death with dignity and as such symbolise the fates of so many in our century. In modern times the medieval demons have taken a different form.

Other sources for this panel emphasise this point. A photograph of refugees in Jordan in 1990 (FIG. 52), and another taken almost a century earlier in 1897 showing the victims of religious strife in Brazil (FIG. 53), have both been referred to by Pacheco. She compares this last photograph to nineteenth-century history painting in its epic scale, and it is likely that the photographer, Flávio de Barros, was consciously attempting to emulate history painters in his work. Pacheco's depictions of helicopters have been taken directly from contemporary photographs of aircraft used in modern conflicts.

The right-hand panel (FIG. 49) shows Anthony writhing on his back before a blasted landscape, while two sphinxes fly above him. The source for the sphinxes is not visual but literary. They originate in Flaubert's version of the legend, and they symbolise the sexual temptation undergone by Saint Anthony in the original story. The sphinx on the left leers triumphantly, and seems positively gleeful at the plight of the struggling figure below. Her power is manifestly evil. Gorgon-like and menacing, she has spiky, sickle-like wings, which originate from ancient images of the east that were assimilated into archaic Greek culture. Her companion, more softly feminine, gazes down with a gentler, almost forgiving, aspect. Her wings are feathered and shaped like those of a bird, a form traditionally used for representations of angels in Christian art. Her power seems to lie in her capacity to bestow benevolence, but only if she should feel minded to do so.

ANA MARIA PACHECO *in the National Gallery*

52 Chris Steele-Perkins, *Refugees in Jordan*, 1990

53 Flávio de Barros, *O resto humano da guerra*, 1897

54 *Luz Eterna* (detail), 1999

Anthony's pose is a rare example in Pacheco's work of a specific quotation. It is related to the painting *Prometheus chained* (FIG. 51), by the Utrecht painter Dirck van Baburen, loaned to the National Gallery for the 'Masters of Light' exhibition and seen by Pacheco as she was developing the composition for *Luz Eterna*. The pose used by Baburen for the Prometheus figure was one which gained popularity in the early seventeenth century. Particularly influential was a painting (also referred to by Pacheco) of Tityus, now in the Museo del Prado, Madrid, by the Neapolitan painter Jusepe Ribera. Similarly, Pacheco's composition for *Luz Eterna* is also of a specific type, one common in Roman Catholic altarpieces of the Counter-Reformation which show earthbound saints experiencing miraculous visions, of Christ, of the Holy Mother or of martyred saints.

Sphinxes however are pagan creatures, representative of feminine power, sexuality and knowledge, all traditionally dangerous concepts in Christian thought. Anthony's torment takes the form of psychological and self-induced guilt. The whole panel accordingly becomes a conflict of male and female, earthbound and heavenly, falling and flying, Christian and pagan.

The left background is a specifically twentieth-century landscape of ruin and destruction. Once again, Pacheco's source is photo-journalism, this time images of Germany and Hiroshima after the war. Burnt-out and bombed buildings loom through the smoke, the barbed-wire fence and the tangled rolls of wire evoke the modern equivalent of the medieval horrors of Bosch. On the right, the hook that hangs from an unseen crane gives the painting another sudden and unexpected contemporary reference, as well as connecting formally with the round shapes of the monks' heads in the left-hand panel.

Queen of Sheba and King Solomon in the Garden of Earthly Delights

'THE STORY OF THE QUEEN OF SHEBA is a very beautiful Biblical text but there are also a lot of apocryphal stories from the Middle East about her. Also, this show is slightly serious, slightly heavy, and I thought it would be nice to have something a bit light-hearted. It is also an opportunity to use colour. The triptych [*Luz Eterna*], because of its subject, needs dark, sombre colours but here I could fully exploit the technique of painting on gesso.'

The setting of *Queen of Sheba and King Solomon in the Garden of Earthly Delights* is the richest and most verdant world that Pacheco has created in her career so far. The idea of a Paradise Garden is rooted in the east and has come to the west through the Judaeo-Christian tradition. 'A garden has enormous implications, not just in terms of the iconography of Christian art. To me, there is this idea of a place where you feel complete and I think that now, when we've lost this sense of completeness, such gardens have to be built up within oneself.'

The two characters in Pacheco's painting enact their meeting in a kind of medieval Garden of Earthly Delights. It is a tangible place, with water, flowers and birds. The porcupine and the monkey, unexpected visitors from the New World, provide Pacheco with a way of staking her own claim to the subject. The choice of flowers is equally precise and deliberate, the artist having made much use of Levi d'Ancona's *The Garden of the Renaissance: Botanical Symbolism in Italian Painting* (Florence, 1977) to learn about the symbolic use of flowers in Renaissance and medieval paintings. 'The point is, though, that through this book, erudite and wonderfully researched, I found that everything is ambivalent. When flowers mean one thing, they can also mean, somewhere else, its opposite.' Pacheco's plants therefore are not meant to be read specifically but carry with them an ambiguity of meaning. The expressions of the two figures are comparable. They tentatively approach each other, both observing and allowing themselves to be observed. Ambivalence is the overwhelming mood.

The story has the Queen of Sheba visiting King Solomon, so this therefore is Solomon's garden. He offers, as host, a precious gift to his visitor, a bejewelled golden box that the Queen studies with a mixture of curiosity and covetousness. Solomon's body language is both sinister and knowing. He is pale-skinned and fully clothed; the Queen, dark and exotic, is obviously naked beneath her translucent robe. She looks at him seductively, one foot suggestively treading on the tail of the peacock, a bird which traditionally symbolises pride but is also associated with Juno and the Virgin Mary, both powerful Queens themselves. The porcupine, with its vicious spines, peeps out from between Solomon's feet. It is a picture about mutual fascination, temptation, danger and entrapment.

55 *Queen of Sheba and King Solomon in the Garden of Earthly Delights*, 1999
Oil on gesso, 242.5 × 168 cm

Beneath the main scene are three predella panels (FIG. 57), a traditional device of Renaissance altarpieces, which show small representations of narratives relevant to the characters in the main picture. 'I would not have done a predella if I had not been at the National Gallery. There is something fascinating and attractive about having a narrative at the bottom, with the main image on the large panel. The predella panels can be time-based, like a film. I have not placed them in linear sequence though, because I like to see them as representations of her dreams.'

According to legend, the Queen of Sheba ruled only half of the land; the other half was ruled by a cruel and rather stupid king. The Queen of Sheba offered herself to him and on the wedding night, chopped off his head. Pacheco tells this story in the first two predella panels. In the left-hand panel, the scheming Queen triumphantly bears away the severed head, and in the centre panel, she kneels before him, offering herself in marriage. The king, his vacuous and dim-witted expression contrasted with his resplendent gilded armour, clenches his fingers and toes in lustful anticipation.

The final panel shows the victorious Queen asleep and dreaming, a dream within a dream. The bird is a hoopoe, Solomon's messenger bird that, according to the legend, travelled the world for him to investigate new territories. It brought him news of the Queen of Sheba and her enormous wealth. Solomon, fascinated, decides to invite her. The hoopoe returns to the Queen with Solomon's letter and drops it into her lap. 'Some of the most beautiful pictures ever made have been of beautiful women sleeping amongst beautiful fabrics and cushions. But for me, the story of King Solomon and the Queen of Sheba is much more about power, these two utterly powerful people encountering one another.'

56 *Queen of Sheba and King Solomon in the Garden of Earthly Delights* (detail), 1999

57 *Queen of Sheba and King Solomon in the Garden of Earthly Delights* (predella panels), 1999

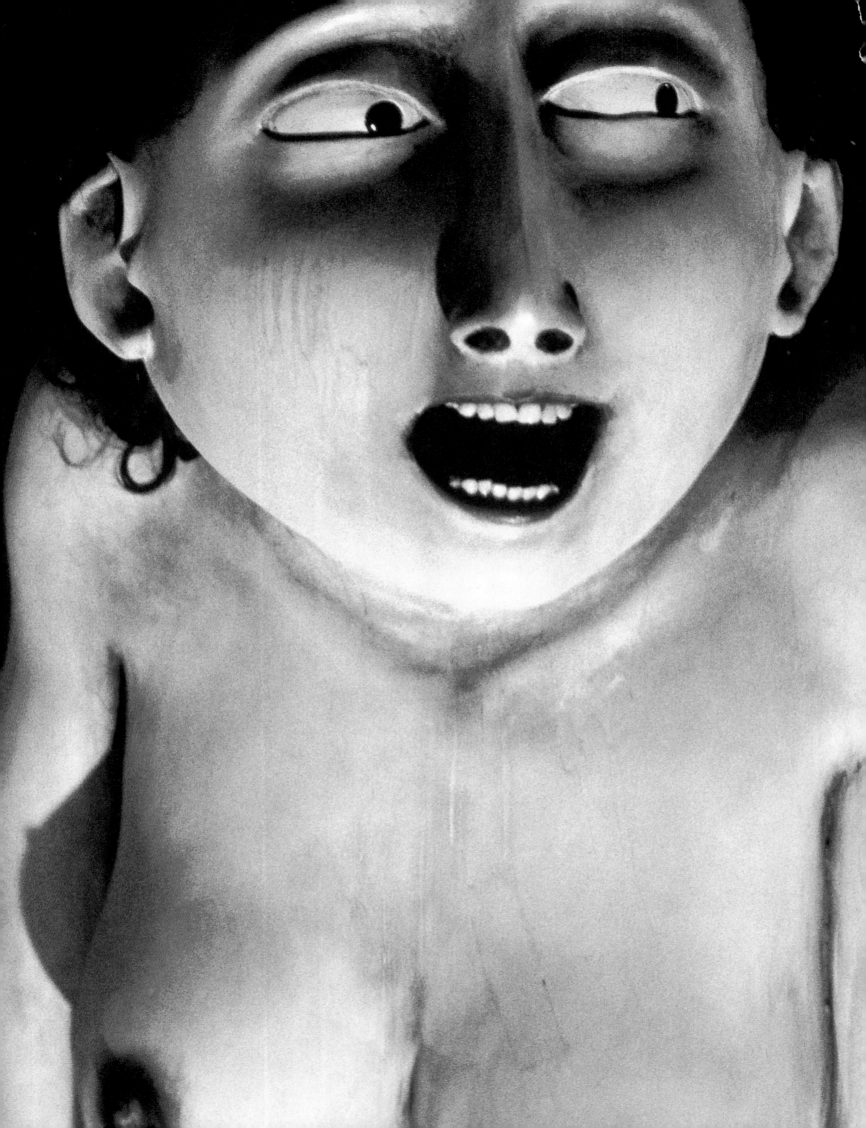

A NOTE ON PACHECO'S TECHNIQUES

Pacheco prepares the panels for her paintings herself. They are made of wood that is then covered with gesso, a mixture of chalk and rabbit-skin glue. The gesso is applied in layers, each one sanded down to a smooth finish before the application of the next. The resultant surface is brilliant white, smooth and hard. The paint is not applied with brushes but is dabbed on with dollies, round balls of tightly bound fabric. This eliminates any trace of handling. The importance of the brushmark in modern painting cannot be overstated, from the Impressionists onwards, up to and including painters like Francis Bacon and Frank Auerbach. While greatly admiring these two painters, she rejects their approach for her own work. 'This notion that *I* make the mark, it's very important to them but I'm not a man', she jokes. 'My preoccupations are somewhere else. I don't care even about signing it. It is perhaps to do with my colonial background but I like things to be well finished. There is this thing about spontaneity, very closely connected with modernism, but I find it impossible.'

58 *Study of Head* (detail, above), 1986
Polychromed wood, height 72.5 cm (exc. base)
Private Collection

The absolute smoothness of Pacheco's surfaces is exactly the opposite to the emphasis on facture and handling that has been a part of so much twentieth-century painting. For Pacheco though, it is only the image that is significant, not the way it is made. 'I want the spectator to confront the imagery directly without anything getting in the way. I do not want people to look at my pictures but to look through them. I want the onlooker to go into them.'

59 *The Three Graces (Figure III)* (detail, left), 1983
Polychromed wood, 195.6 × 170.2 × 123.2 cm
Wolverhampton Art Gallery

The whiteness of the gesso ground has a profound effect on the colours. The pictures are painted in oil, a medium that allows light to reflect off the surface but also to pass through to and reflect off the white ground. Once the composition has been established, many successive layers of colour are applied to bring the surface to a very high degree of finish. Once dried, the artist uses a very fine glass paper to rub down the surface, before applying a layer of pure bleached beeswax. Consequently, Pacheco's colours have the same qualities of richness and saturation that is found in paintings by early Netherlandish artists of the fifteenth century.

60 Tubes of paint in Pacheco's studio at the National Gallery

The sculptures are given a similar high finish. They are initially blocked out with a chain saw, then details such as heads, hands and feet are carved, while much of the drapery is worked with a chain saw and then burnt with a blow-torch. The colour, mixed with diluted emulsion paint and the same kind of gesso that is used for the paintings, is applied with cotton buds.

Pacheco's figures are generalised types, yet each, within certain conventions, is an individual character. The porcelain teeth, each inserted separately, are obtained from a dental supplier, and play an important role in giving the figures their identity. 'Teeth give a very specific look to a face, because people's teeth are always different. Talking to a dentist I learnt that there are some basic shapes of teeth but that the way they are set in someone's mouth is always individual to that person. The look of the teeth can change a face enormously.' There is also of course a close affinity with sculptures such as African tribal masks, that are set with real teeth.

CHRONOLOGY

COLLECTIONS INCLUDE

Birmingham Museums and Art Gallery
Hat Hill Sculpture Foundation, Chichester
British Museum, London
Arts Council, London
Tate Gallery, London
Victoria and Albert Museum, London
Whitworth Art Gallery, Manchester
Norwich Castle Museum
Castle Museum, Nottingham
Oldham Art Gallery
Ashmolean Museum, Oxford
Harris Museum and Art Gallery, Preston
South East Arts Collection
The Unilever Collection
Wolverhampton Art Gallery
Herzog Anton Ulrich-Museum, Braunschweig, Germany
Setagaya Art Museum, Tokyo, Japan
Museum of Contemporary Graphic Art, Fredrikstad, Norway
Cincinnati Art Museum, Ohio, USA

SELECTED BIBLIOGRAPHY

Helen Boorman and Ian Starsmore, *Ana Maria Pacheco –
    Sculpture, Paintings, Drawings and Prints 1980–1989*,
    Pratt Contemporary Art, 1989.
Andrew Brighton, *The Work of Ana Maria Pacheco*,
    Pratt Contemporary Art, 1994.
Frances Carey, *The Prints of Ana Maria Pacheco*, Print Quarterly,
    vol. V, no. 3, 1988.
David Elliott and Paul Hills, *Ana Maria Pacheco, In Illo Tempore*,
    Pratt Contemporary Art, 1994.
Vivian Schelling and Simon Willmoth, *Ana Maria Pacheco –
    Twenty Years of Printmaking*, Pratt Contemporary Art, 1994.
George Szirtes, *Rites and melodies. The Work of Ana Maria Pacheco*,
    Contemporary Art, vol. II, no. 4, Winter 1994/5.
George Szirtes, *Ana Maria Pacheco's The Longest Journey*,
    Pratt Contemporary Art, 1996.

BRIEF BIOGRAPHY

1943	Born in Goiás, Brazil.
1960–4	Bachelor of Arts in Sculpture, University of Goiás, Brazil. Degree in Music, Federal University of Goiás.
1965	Studies in Music and Education, University of Brazil, Rio de Janeiro.
1966–73	Lecturer at the School of Fine Arts and the School of Architecture, University of Goiás. Lecturer at the Institute of Art, Federal University of Goiás.
1973–5	British Council Scholarship to the Slade School of Fine Art, London.
1985–9	Head of Fine Art, Norwich School of Art, Norfolk.
1996	Appointed Fourth Associate Artist at the National Gallery, London (1997–2000).

SELECTED EXHIBITIONS

1980	Institute of Contemporary Arts, London, 'Women's Images of Men', group show, touring (Sculpture).
1982	Hayward Annual, London.
1983	Ikon Gallery, Birmingham, one person show (Sculpture, Drawings, Paintings and Prints).
1985	International Contemporary Art Fair (Pratt Contemporary Art), London, one person show (Sculpture and Drawings). Cornerhouse, Manchester, 'Human Interest', group show (Sculpture).
1989–90	Artsite Gallery and St John's Catholic Church, Bath, one person show (Sculpture, Paintings, Drawings and Prints), touring.
1991	Camden Arts Centre, London, 'Some Exercise of Power', one person show (Sculpture and Drawings). Museum of Modern Art, Oxford, 'Some Exercise of Power', one person show (Sculpture and Drawings).
1992	Trondhjems Kunstforening, Trondheim, Norway, one person show (Sculpture). Winchester Cathedral, 'Trilogy', (Sculpture and Drawings).
1993	Oslo Kunstforening, Norway, one person show (Sculpture and Prints).
1994	Norwich Castle Museum, Norfolk, one person show (Sculpture and Prints). The Gas Hall, Birmingham Museums and Art Gallery, 'The Longest Journey', one person show (Sculpture and Paintings).
1994–6	'Twenty Years of Printmaking', one person show (Prints), touring.
1995	Ormeau Baths Gallery, Belfast, Northern Ireland, inaugural exhibition (Sculpture and Prints). Sculpture at Goodwood/Hat Hill Sculpture Foundation. Work sited (*Requiem*) and gallery exhibition (*Man and His Sheep*).
1996	The Chicago Art Fair, USA (Sculpture). The Trout Gallery (Weiss Center for the Arts), Dickinson College, Pennsylvania, USA, one person show (Sculpture and Prints).
1997	Old Jail Art Center, Albany, Texas, one person show (Sculpture and Prints). Aberystwyth Arts Centre, Wales, one person show (Sculpture and Prints). Wrexham Library Arts Centre, one person show (Sculpture and Prints). Wolverhampton Art Gallery, 'The Body Politic', group show (Sculpture).
1998	Derby Museums and Art Gallery, 'The Body Politic', group show (Sculpture).
1999	Kilkenny Arts Festival, Ireland, one person show (Sculpture and Paintings). National Gallery, London.

ANA MARIA PACHECO *in the National Gallery*